Talking About

Racism

Nicola Edwards

Chrysalis Education

Distributed in the United States by
Smart Apple Media
1980 Lookout Drive
North Mankato, Minnesota 56003

Copyright © Chrysalis Books PLC 2003

ISBN 1-93233-306-1

The Library of Congress control number 2003102417

Editorial manager: Joyce Bentley
Senior editor: Sarah Nunn
Picture researchers: Terry Forshaw, Lois Charlton
Designer: Wladek Szechter
Editor: Kate Phelps
Consultant: Dr Ute Navidi, Head of Policy, ChildLine

Printed in China

The pictures used in this book do not show the actual people named in the text.

Foreword

People are not born racists. Racist behavior is learned, and racist attitudes are based on ignorance and fear of others. Through vivid, topical examples, **Talking About Racism** shows that racism hurts people. Children can hurt each other by name-calling as well as physical attacks. Making fun of or bullying other children because they look, speak, or behave differently is also unfair.

Talking About Racism enables adults, teachers, and children to talk about racism and inequality and helps tackle racist attitudes before they become entrenched. It reinforces schools' anti-bullying strategies by emphasizing respect and friendship. Speaking out about racism takes courage, and by identifying someone they can talk to safely—a trusted adult, a friend of their own age, or a helpline—children take the first step towards finding help for themselves or their friends.

But **Talking About Racism** goes beyond confronting racist bullying at school. Highlighting the feelings of refugee and asylum-seeking children exemplifies the global context. By discussing racist abuse shouted at football matches to anti-racist demonstrations, this book reflects wider social attitudes.

Informative and thought-provoking, the **Talking About** series tackles some disturbing aspects of contemporary society: racism, domestic violence, divorce, eating problems, and bullying. Adults often try to protect children from these problems or believe they will not understand. Taking children through a series of situations they can identify with—using words and images—also means offering alternative ways of resolving conflict. Each book shows that even very young children are not passive observers or victims. They want to make sense of their world and act to make life better for themselves, their families, and other children.

Ute Navidi, Head of Policy, ChildLine (a U.K. helpline for children in distress)

Contents

What is racism?

Racism is treating someone differently or unfairly because of the color of their skin or the country they come from. Racism often leads to **bullying**.

These children shouted insults at Jade because she is black.

When Louis was new at school,
children bullied him
because he is French.

Racist bullies pick on people and call them
names. They may attack people by punching
or kicking them, or throwing things at them.

Making fun

Children often pick on others they see as being different in some way. They may wear different clothes or eat different foods because of their family background or religion.

Yasmin was proud to be a **Muslim**. But she didn't like it when some people stared at her and her family in the street.

Children made fun of Ali.
They didn't like the food he brought
to school.

Children sometimes laugh at things they
find strange or unusual. But what seems
like harmless fun to one person can
make someone else very upset.

It's no joke

Sometimes, when bullies are told off about their behavior, they say that they were just playing around. They try to make people think that they didn't mean any harm.

Robert thought it was funny to laugh at his friend Conor's Irish accent.

James was treated unfairly by children who knew nothing about him except what he looked like.

They say the person they were bullying can't take a joke. But racist bullying makes people feel sad, **lonely**, and frightened.

Bullying is always wrong. Don't be a bully.

Not just in school

Racism is a big problem in the world today. It causes pain and suffering to many people. Racists think that they are more important than others who come from a different **culture**.

IN MEMORY OF
STEPHEN LAWRENCE
13.9.1974
22.4.1993
MAY HE REST IN PEACE

Stephen Lawrence was a young, black man in London, England who was killed in the street by a **gang** of racists.

Racists hate these other people and think they have the right to attack them.

This girl from a **refugee** family had to leave her home and come to a country where she did not feel welcome.

Why are people racist?

People are not born racists. Racism is an attitude that develops in some people as they grow up. It is often learned from family or friends.

These marchers are complaining about people from other countries coming to live in Britain.

Racists in Britain set fire to this shop owned by an Asian family.

Racists are ignorant of other cultures and often frightened by what they do not understand.

Safe at home?

Everyone has the right to feel safe.
But sometimes racists try to upset and frighten
people in their homes by smashing their
windows or spraying nasty messages on walls.

Sometimes racists
can make people feel very worried and
afraid even in their own homes.

Racists sometimes attack buildings where people **worship** too.

This **synagogue** is a holy building for Jewish people. It was attacked by racists.

Racist attacks are against the **law**. Police officers try to catch the racists.

Racism in the street

People often have to cope with racism while they are trying to get on with their everyday lives.

Ross was worried about being bullied by racists on the way home from school. His friend, Sean, said they could travel back together, in a group of friends.

Some soccer players in Britain say they experience racist **abuse** at games.

Racists are **cowards**. They need to feel part of a group. Racist gangs may throw things at people in the street, punch them, or damage their cars— simply because they look or speak differently.

How does it feel?

Racist bullying can make children feel sad and lonely. They may feel that they can't tell anyone at home about it because they don't want to worry or upset them. Children may even feel angry with their parents for giving them their skin color.

Racist bullies made Imrie feel very sad and angry.

Bullies tried to make Lisa feel ashamed that her dad is black.

Being bullied can make people feel **ashamed** and worthless.

Sometimes people that are bullied may pretend to be ill, refuse to go to school, or refuse to go out to play because of the bullying.

Don't stand for it

Racism is wrong and no one should have to put up with it. Racist bullies like people to see them bullying someone. It makes them feel important.

These people are marching to show that they are against racism.

If you are being bullied,
it is brave to tell someone. It is not
telling tales.

People can help to stop bullies by refusing
to stand by and watch it happen.

If you are bullied, or if you
see bullying in school, tell
an adult you **trust**.

Beating racism

Teachers know that racist bullying can happen in schools. They must help children who are bullied. Principals can let everyone in the school know that racism is wrong and that it is not allowed.

The principal told the children that they are all equal and that everyone has a part to play in stamping out racist bullying in school.

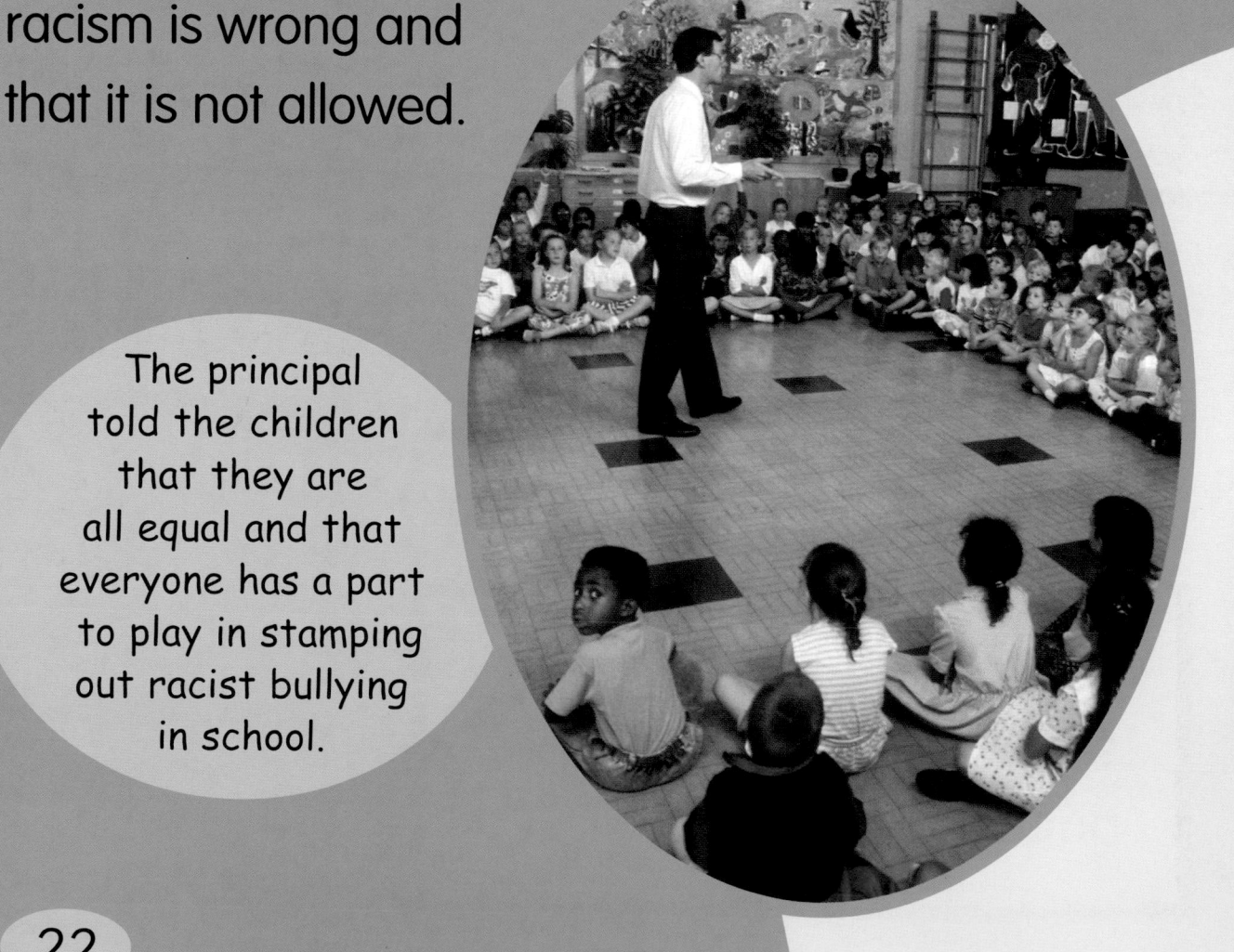

Bullies are less likely to pick on people who look **confident** and **determined**.

Children can help stop racist bullying by showing **respect** to others and ignoring racists.

If someone tries to bully you, shout "GO AWAY!," and then tell a teacher.

Learning from each other

Racism sometimes happens because people do not understand or respect how other people live or what they believe.

These children enjoyed finding out how **Hindu** people celebrate **Diwali**.

Balraj invited his Irish friend, Caitlin, to his sister's wedding.

People are happier when they offer each other friendship and respect.

The world is a better place because it is made up of billions of different people, each with their own history, background, and personality.

Teamwork

Everyone is different, with their own special strengths and **talents**. It makes people happy when others show them respect by being polite and friendly.

Great things can happen when people respect each other's differences and value each other's talents.

These soccer players work as a team and show respect for each other.

Think about what makes you special and what you like about your friends.

Everyone has the right to live without fear. People can work together to fight against racism.

Good friends

Some children get very upset when their friends are bullied by racists. Children who have been bullied say their friends helped them to cope and change things for the better.

Children can work together to build a future without racism.

The world
is a happier place
when people of all
races can love one
another and live
together
without fear.

It's important for everyone
to feel that they have friends
who care about them and
respect them.

Words to remember

abuse Words or actions that harm someone.

ashamed Feeling bad, as if you have done something wrong.

bullying Hurting someone or making them feel sad.

confident Feeling as if you can do anything.

coward Someone who acts as if they are brave when they are in a crowd but who is afraid when on their own.

culture The ideas, skills, arts, and way of life of a group of people.

determined Strongly intending to do something.

Diwali An important festival in the Hindu religion.

gang A group of people.

Hindu A follower of the religion Hinduism.

laws The rules which people in a country follow.

lonely Feeling sad, as if you have no friends.

Muslim A follower of the religion of Islam.

refugees People who have left their own country because it is not safe.

respect To think well of people and be polite to them.

synagogue A building where Jewish people worship.

talents Skills, what someone is good at doing.

trust Feeling that someone won't let you down.

worship Praying and giving thanks to God.

Organizations, helplines, and websites

Anti-Defamation League
Has 30 regional offices in the U.S. (and three overseas). Deals with wide range of issues, from anti-semitism to combating hate. A catalog of resources for the classroom includes books for young people about extraordinary African-Americans, Asian Americans, Hispanic Americans, Native Americans.
www.ade.org/

Antiracist.com
Website of the Canadian Anti-racism Education and Research Society (CAERS) which exposes and combats racism. Has news features, details of anti-racist events, information about laws.
P.O. Box 2783
Vancouver, British Columbia
V6A 2E2
www.antiracist.com

Let's End All Racism Now (LEARN)
U.S. educational program for children and adults, including special "topic of the month" discussions, and comments by participants.
www.learnart.com/

National Association for the Advancement of Colored People (NAACP)
Works for the protection of civil rights of African Americans and other minorities.
4805 Mt. Hope Drive
Baltimore, Maryland
21215
24-hour hotline: (410) 521-4939
www.naacp.org/

Say NO to Racism
Website of the New Brunswick Human Rights Commission. Explores what is racism, what is meant by prejudice, what can I do to stop racism, links to other sources of information.
P.O. Box 6000,
Fredericton, NB,
Canada, E3B 5H1
www.gnb.ca/hrc-cdp/e/sayno.htm

Index